ACOUSTIC GUITAR BEGINNER'S GUIDE

FOREWORD

The following book for beginners will give you the tools you need to teach yourself the basics of playing guitar, whether or not you already read music. Whether you are planning to start a band, already play in a band, or want to play guitar to accompany your own or others' singing, you will find the basics here in this book.

The guitar is one of the most common instruments in the world of music. There are different types of acoustic guitar: standard wooden guitars with nylon strings, wooden guitars with steel strings, guitars with electro-acoustic pickups, flat-top guitars, 12-string guitars and even left-handed guitars. Most important when learning guitar is knowledge of the chords. A singer, or an instrument like a trumpet, cannot produce chords, only individual notes. This is where the guitar has a distinct advantage. This book covers chord fingering in detail, as well as differing strumming techniques for playing songs, and rhythm patterns for accompaniment.

The included CD serves as a training partner. It is particularly useful for giving you an idea of how each chord, pattern and song should sound.

To make certain terms clearer for the reader, I have used the following notation throughout the book: the dash is used when dealing with composite constructions of major or minor, e.g. major-scale. Capitalized or lowercase letters correspond to the conventions of international notation, e.g.: E-major = E, A-minor = Am. The chord and note notation meet international standards for music and text.

CONTENTS

THE INSTRUMENT

Parts of the Guitar

As an instrument, the guitar is very old. Guitar-like instruments date back to three thousand years ago in ancient Greece. The guitar belongs to an instrument group called chordophones. The name does not have anything to do with chords; it means "necked box lute". Guitar strings sound over a wooden box, one which is not square, but gently rounded and convex. The guitar's means of sound production make it a stringed instrument, and the playing style makes it a plucked instrument. The latter is true even if you are mostly playing with a pick.

Related instruments include the ukulele, the lute, the banjo, the mandolin and the lap steel guitar.

The guitar consists of the body (this is the rounded wooden box, which acts as a sound-box), the neck (where the strings run) and the head. There are six keys in the head of the guitar for tuning the strings.

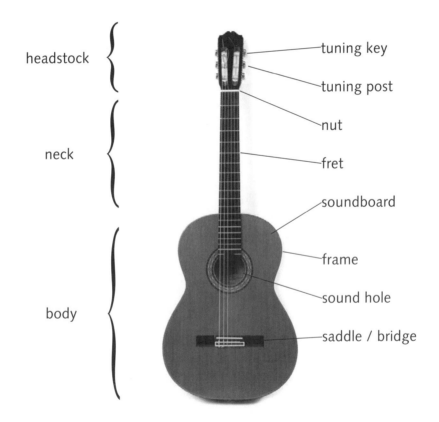

headstock

neck

body

tuning key

tuning post

nut

fret

soundboard

frame

sound hole

saddle / bridge

Playing Position

The Classical Position

In this position, the player sits forward on a chair with his or her left foot on a small stool. You can also use brackets called 'supports' that attach to the underside of the instrument frame and sit on top of your left thigh. Both of these positions look a bit "uncool". The stool makes it look like you are sitting in class, and you will find you rarely have the support around when you need it. For our purposes, this position is somewhat impractical.

The Relaxed Position

Lots of guitarists prefer a relaxed sitting position while playing. You can place the guitar on your right thigh and support it with your right arm. Play around with this position and figure out what is comfortable for you. You can also cross your left leg over the right if that works better. More than anything, it is important to stay loose and relaxed while you practice. Both hands have to be free, the right hand for picking, and the left hand for fingering.

The Standing Position

Especially in the Rock and Pop music world, the guitar is played while standing. You will need a secure strap, which comes in hundreds of variations. It is important to ensure that the instrument does not hang too low or you could have problems playing chords. If you have trouble fitting a guitar strap to your instrument, a retailer or instrument maker can help you out. You can also just hold the guitar tightly between your elbow and upper body. The standing position is very useful for singers who accompany themselves.

Tuning

It is annoying, but you have to do it. An out of tune guitar just sounds awful, ruining your ear for the music and ensuring that nobody will want to listen to you play.

So let's get right into tuning:
As you know, the guitar has six strings (as is always the case, with a few exceptions) and these strings all have names and numbers. Starting with the thickest and lowest sounding string, the sixth:

6th string = E-string (the low E-string or the "fat" E-string)
5th string = A-string
4th string = D-string
3rd string = g-string
2nd string = b-string
1st string = e-string (the high e-string or the 'skinny' e-string)

The easiest way to tune your guitar is to use an electronic tuning device. There are also tuning forks, pitch pipes and other methods you can use. Do not rely on those, however – buy yourself an electronic tuner. Other methods are complicated and more trouble than they are worth. An electronic tuning device is always on pitch, and is quick and easy to use.

TIP: A tuning device measures pitch with incredible accuracy. Guitars are generally made from wood, a material that 'shifts', expanding in the heat and contracting in the cold. Add rain and damp, and things get even worse.
In some cases, cheaper instruments may bow slightly at the neck. If this happens, you may have to adjust the tuning on your guitar (see further information after the text 'reflexive tuning'). If you do not yet have a tuning device, you can tune your guitar using the accompanying CD and the following track numbers.

 Track 32
Tuning note E-string

 Track 35
Tuning note g-string

 Track 33
Tuning note A-string

 Track 36
Tuning tone b-string

Track 34
Tuning note D-string

Track 37
Tuning note e-string

In the interests of full disclosure, I will also show you here how to reflexively tune the guitar, since there are times when you will not have a tuning fork or tuning device around (although that should not happen – from now on, these things are part of your guitar playing tool kit and should always be close at hand). If you assume that the lowest E-string is in tune, you can use your left hand to hold the string down on the 5th fret and use the resulting note to bring the A-string into tune. The 5th fret of the E-string plays an identical A-note to the A-string. After tuning the A-string as described above, you can move on to tune the remaining strings in the same way. The following table shows which string and which fret you have to play.

This is how to reflexively tune the guitar:

- Open A-string in tune with the 5th fret on the E-string
- Open D-string with the 5th fret on the A-string
- Open g-string with the 5th fret on the D-string
- Open b-string with the 4th fret on the g-string
- Open e-string with the 5th fret on the b-string

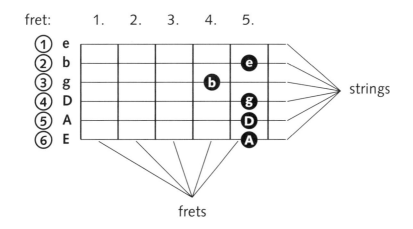

RIGHT HAND — LEFT HAND

The Left Hand

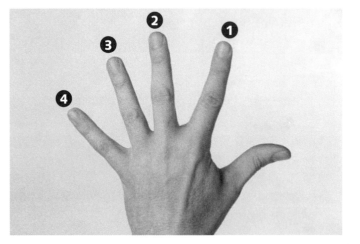

With guitar chords (fingering) you can accompany songs on your guitar. The chords are played with the left hand (fingering hand) on the fret board of the guitar neck. To indicate which finger should be used, we give each finger a number:

Index finger (1), middle finger (2), ring finger (3), pinky finger (4).

The fingers should be placed parallel to the frets. Both finger joints have to sag to the left a little – do not let them push inwards.

The thumb is used to support your left hand. Place your thumb on the back of the guitar neck.

The thumb should not extend out over the fret board. Ideally the thumb is placed opposite the 2nd finger, so that your four fingers and thumb create a rough circle.

TIP: You need a lot less strength to push down on a guitar string than most beginners think. Do not press too hard!

The Right Hand

The guitar strings are plucked or struck with the fingers of the right hand (the picking hand) or a pick.

In classic sheet music you will frequently see p, i, m, a, for the Spanish names of the fingers: thumb, Span. pulgar (p), index finger, Span. indice (I), middle finger, Span. medio (m), ring finger, Span. anula (a). In this book, I use the easier-to-remember English initials:

Thumb (T),

Index finger (I),

Middle finger (M),

Ring Finger (R).

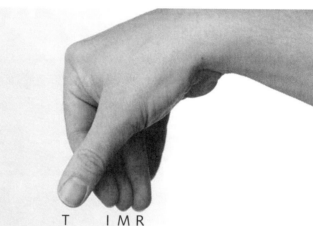

There is a best position for plucking the strings with your hand: use the right thumb for the low E-string, the A-string, and, on occasion, for the D-string as well. The thumb strikes the strings 'downwards'. The index finger plucks the g-string, the middle finger the b-string, and the ring finger the e-string 'upwards' toward the palm of your hand.

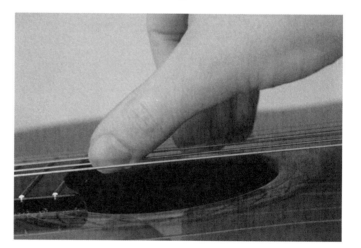

You should pluck the strings using your fingertips. If your fingernails are long enough, you can also pluck with them. With this 'nail technique' the sound is clearer and louder. Using a mix of finger tip and nail gives a rounded 'classical' sound.

The Pick

Chords can be strummed with either the right hand or with a pick. The pick is held, as shown in the picture, between the index finger and the thumb.

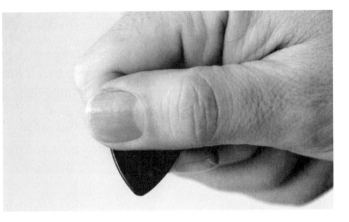

There are two different strumming directions. The musical notation for simultaneous strumming of all or multiple strings is shown below:

From the thickest to thinnest string = down-stroke,

From the thinnest to the thickest string = up-stroke.

You can produce uniform up and down strokes by moving your right forearm and wrist. Try out the following exercise. Try to keep your strokes (up and down) as regular and even as possible.

Track 01

THE BEAT

Notation

You will find the time signature at the beginning of a piece of music, directly after the clef sign. At the end of each measure is a bar line. A double bar separates larger groups of beats (song segments or parts) from one another. Segments which are to be played more than once are represented by a repeat sign. If something different is to be played at the end of the repeated phrase, so called Volta brackets are used. The first time, the contents of Bracket 1 are played. The second time through, the contents of Bracket 2 are played. At the end of the section is a double bar, with the second line is somewhat thicker, or a final stroke.

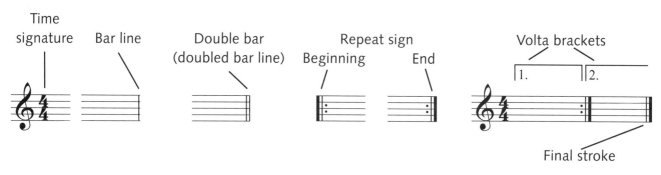

4/4 Time

Every musical piece is divided into meters. Quarter time is the meter that comes most naturally to most people. The beat is derived from walking pace, or, more specifically, from marching. Four quarters make up one whole, as I am sure you have learnt that in math class. It is exactly the same in music. Four quarters make up one bar and four bars make up a musical phrase. 4x4 phrases (16 phrases) generally make up one song. Exception: in Blues music 3x4 (12) phrases make up one song.
At the beginning of a piece, you will see two numbers. The top number shows the number of equal beats into which the bar is separated. The bottom number shows the note value of the individual beats.
So, if you see 4/4 next to the clef, it means that you count four beats per bar, and that each beat is worth a quarter note. Ninety percent of all popular songs are played in this time signature.
The 'down' beats are played by the bass and the big drum. We guitarists play the 'up' beats: 2 and 4.
To prevent us from missing the beat (or the rhythm of the song), we count the quarters of a bar while playing. It does not matter whether you do this out loud or silently, as long as your count remains steady.

The count in 4/4-time:

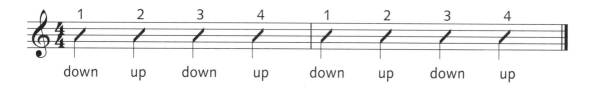

Other Time Signatures

There are plenty of other time signatures, e.g. 3/4-time, 2/4-time, 6/8-time, cut time, and a variety of composite time signatures from the folk music of other cultures. Especially important for playing songs, however, are 2/4-time, 3/4-time and 6/8-time. Once again: what you count is the top number of the time signature. The bottom number shows which unit of the beat to count in.

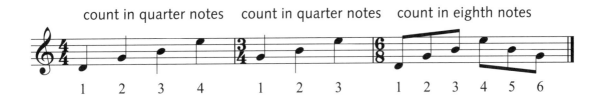

READING MUSIC

The Open Strings

I won't lie: you can play guitar without learning to read music. But reading music makes it much more interesting, because you will be able to learn and practice more songs. More than anything, reading music allows you to pick up a piece of paper and remember how to play an old song just by glancing at the music. That is why some people call reading music "sight reading". Sheet music is made up of written signs for the sounds that you play, taken down on a piece of paper. Thanks to written music, you can learn to play songs that you have never heard before. You can give your friends an example of how a song should sound by playing the melody for them, and you will not run into trouble just because someone brings new music with them, or if the singer cannot quite decide which song he or she is going to sing.

All notes are written on a staff that consists of five lines and four spaces. The lines as well as the spaces are counted from the bottom up.

Now, to the instrument itself. We do not need the left hand just yet. Bring the right hand to the correct position over the strings and play one note at a time, switching between the index finger and middle finger. If you are playing with a pick, switch between upward and downward strokes of the pick for each note.

We will begin with the high e-string and pay attention to note placement, in this case in the space between the fourth and fifth lines.

Next is the b-string. This note is right in the middle on the third line.

The symbol for the note 'g' sits on the second line.

The note for the pitch 'D' sits underneath the first line. This string can be played with the thumb or with your fingers. Since we will be playing melodies to begin with, it is better to use your finger.

The note for the pitch 'A' sits in the middle of the second ledger line under the staff. This string should always be played with your thumb.

The note for the pitch 'E' sits underneath the third ledger line. This is the lowest note on the guitar.

TIP: A mnemonic is the best way to remember the name of each open string, e.g. Eddie-Ate-Dynamite-Good-Bye-Eddie. The first letters of each word in the previous sentence are the names of the guitar strings from the low 'E' onwards. Of course, you can always invent your own mnemonic sentence to help you remember.

You can also play the strings in a different order, see page 9 "The Right Hand." Here is an example:

see page 9 "The Right Hand."

Track 02

The Fingered Notes

Now we are going to start using the left hand. We place it on the fret board, with the fingers hovering over the neck and the thumb supporting it. The fingers spread out a little so that every finger sits just in front of the fret near the left edge. If the strings clang while playing, your fingers are placed in the middle of the fret, or too far to the right.

You can play two natural notes on every string. The g-string is an exception, as it only has one natural note. The following bars have numbers above the music indicating which fingers you should use to play the notes. A '0' means playing an open string.

Track 03

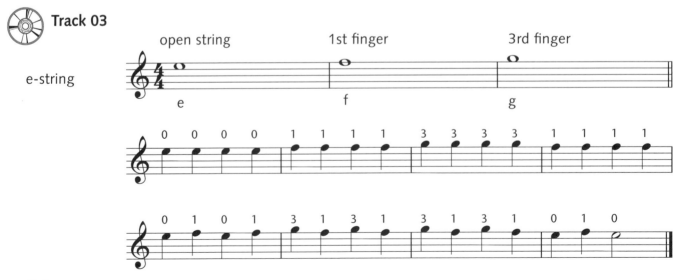

Track 04

b-string

open string   1st finger   3rd finger

Track 05

g-string

open string   2nd finger

Track 06

D-string

open string   2nd finger   3rd finger

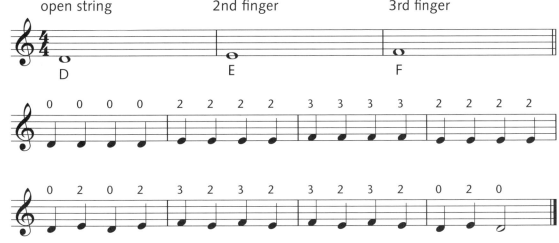

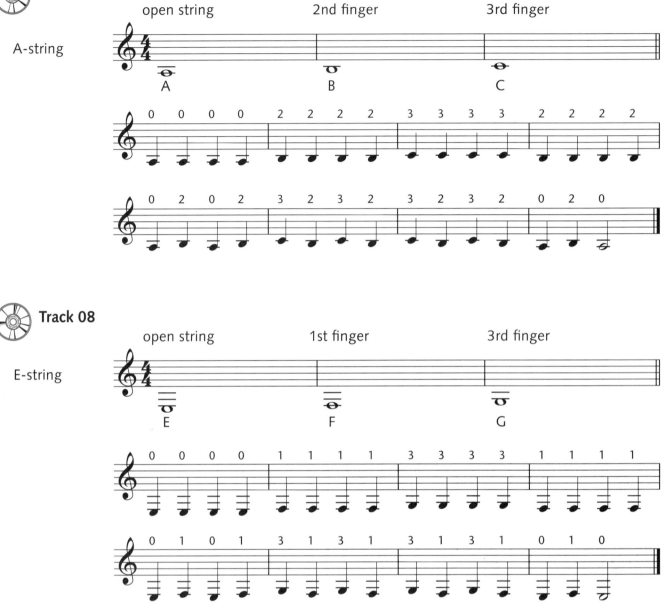

You can now play a total of seventeen notes. You should play 3 x forwards and backwards through these notes several times a day, every day, before actually beginning to play songs on your guitar. The first time through, play every note 4 x, then 2 x, and finally 1 x. Following this section, you will see a summary of the notes from the lowest E-string to the 3rd fret of the highest e-string. To make this summary easier to navigate, we have placed the number of the strings in brackets above the notes. See also page 6 "Tuning."

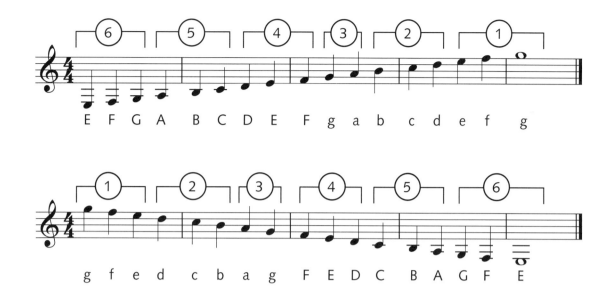

TIP: There are two short sentences which make it easy to remember the names of the notes: "every-good-boy-does-fine" for the notes on the lines, and "f-a-c-e" for the notes in the spaces. You can use these mnemonics or make up your own to help you remember which notes are on and in between the lines of the staff.

The Key Signature

The key signature is really a shorthand method for writing accidentals. It is used to show the player that the notes in a piece are not played in their usual position, but either a half-step higher or lower. The notes that result are called 'chromatic'. Some people call them 'semitones'. The reason there are seven diatonic notes (a progression of whole and semitones, see also page 19 "Scales") but only five chromatic notes, is that there is not a whole tone but rather a semitone between the 3rd and 4th degree and the 7th and 8th degree of the scale. The semitones effectively create an intermediate step between those natural notes that have a whole note between them. This is easy to see when looking at a keyboard: there are seven white and five black keys which repeat in a continuing pattern. All twelve notes together form the chromatic scale, with a semitone between each note on the scale.

♯   If the natural notes are raised by a semitone, the word 'sharp' is added and the note is played one fret higher than the natural note of the same name. A symbol like a small slanted grate, the sharp symbol, is added after the symbol for the note. My students call the sharp symbol the 'fly swatter'. The sharp symbol reminds us that the natural note should be played one fret higher, e.g. a# = a sharp, or c# = c sharp.

♭   If the natural note is diminished by a semitone, the word 'flat' is added and the note is played one fret lower than the natural note of the same name. The letter 'b', the flat, is added after the symbol for the note. My students call the flat symbol the 'backpack'. It helps us remember that the natural note should be played one fret lower. The note is 'brought down' by this sign. Exceptions: A becomes Ab (spoken 'A flat'), E becomes Eb (spoken 'E flat') and B becomes Bb (spoken 'B flat').

♮   The accidentals 'only' apply to the bar where they appear, and will be repeated in the next bar if they apply there as well. If the accidental no longer applies to notes within the same bar, it is cancelled by the natural sign.

All the notes that you can play on the guitar's neck, from the 1st to the 12th fret, are semitones. The twelve frets for each guitar string represent the twelve semitones in an octave, and the upper octave is complete at the 12th fret. It is sometimes marked on your guitar with two points on or above the fret board. This is also where the wooden body of the guitar begins. After that, there are a few more frets running over the body, normally six. These frets do not matter much if you are playing songs.

An example: The twelve frets on the high e-string represent twelve chromatic semitones (one octave).

The placement of the notes is exactly the same on the other five strings, but begins with the notes for each respective open string. The notes on the high and low E-strings have the same names, but differ in sound by two octaves.

Scales

The naturals (diatonic notes) repeat themselves in low and high ranges, creating the eight notes of an octave. The word 'Octave' comes from the Latin word octava (eighth). The eight notes contained in an octave are called a 'scale'. You can build a scale starting from any of the twelve semitones.

To begin with, we will look at the major scales, which are all constructed identically: whole note-whole note-semitone-whole note-whole note-whole note-semitone.

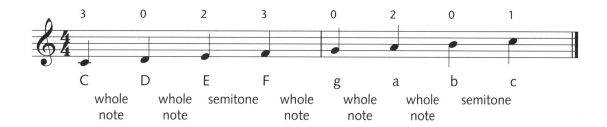

The deciding feature in every major scale is the position of the semitones. There is always a semitone breaking up the row of whole notes between the third and fourth degree and the seventh and eighth degree. This central, basic rule of music makes it necessary to add notes that can be raised or diminished. The most important scales for guitarists are the so-called 'sharp' scales, or melodies with a constantly increasing number of sharps.

The most important scale is the C-major scale.

After that we continue further upwards through the sharps, first to G-major.

D-major is one of the most important scales for the guitar.

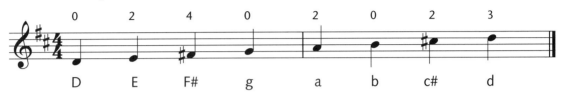

A-major is also quite common in songs for the guitar.

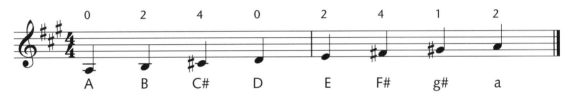

E-major has a total of four sharps. This key is difficult to play, but sounds great.

Major and Minor

There is also a second musical mode, or the 'minor' mode. Major and minor are opposites. The two modes come up often when dealing with music. Major, the 'hard' mode, is generally considered bright and clear, while the softer minor mode is considered melancholy and sad.
These classifications are not necessarily all that accurate anymore. There are fast Rock songs performed in the minor mode, and deeply tragic ballads in the major. Today, much more depends on the song's tempo (speed) and the emotions (feelings, spirit).

Scales can be played in major or minor keys. You have already seen some of the major scales. The difference between the two modes is the note in the third place (the "third"), which can be raised or lowered. If it is raised, the scale is a major triad. If it is lowered, the scale is a minor triad. Just like the major scales, there are twelve different minor scales. You can find more information in the chapter "The Cadence" (see page 46).

Here are the most useful minor scales:

We will begin with A-minor.

Then go to D-minor.

Finally, we will get to know E-minor.

The Rhythm

Before we start off with the first melodies, we have to come to terms with rhythm. The rhythm is a combination of long or short notes and determines how the piece will sound throughout. The tempo of a piece, which is noted above the first time signature by the metronome mark or, more commonly today, in 'bpm' (beats per minute), determines the speed at which the rhythm plays. For example, the metronome mark '60' or the entry 'bpm = 60' means that 60 beats (quarter notes) are to be played per minute. That means exactly one beat per second.

The longest note that we have to get to know is a whole note. It is four quarters long and takes up an entire bar. That is also how we get the name: whole note = whole bar.

You play this note on the count of 1 and count evenly up to 4. The following note values become progressively smaller (shorter) by half. Two half-notes will be followed by four quarter-notes. It is exactly like sharing a pizza: 1 whole pizza just for you, 2 halves of the pizza for two people, 4 quarters for four people. Once we reach the eighth notes, we have to divide up the quarter notes we are counting by using the word 'and', as in, "and a 1 and 2 and 3 and 4." In the music you will see a plus sign (+) in place of the word 'and.' Once we reach the sixteenth notes, we have to play two notes for each number (1,2,3,4) and each 'and' that we count.

Whole note: no filling (white), thick, no stem

Half note: no filling (white), normal, with stem

Quarter note: filled in, with stem

Eighth note: filled in, with a flag or beam

Sixteenth note: filled in, with two beams or two flags

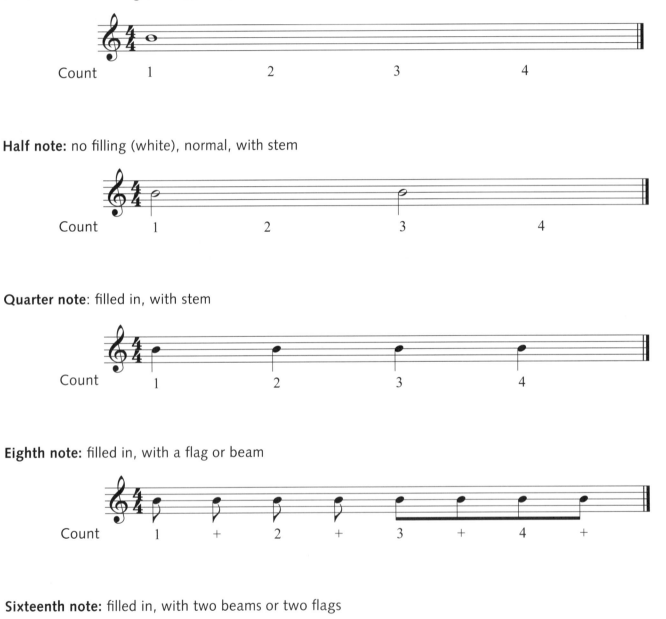

Rests

There are also pauses in music notation, called rests. They match the value of the notes exactly and should be handled just as you would handle notes, by counting them out.

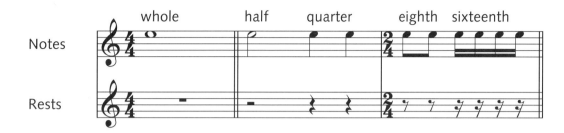

Dotted Notes and Ties

A dot placed after a note lengthens the note by one half of its value. For example, a half-note with a dot after it indicates that we have to count to 2 (the value of the note), plus 1 (the value of the dot), for a total count of 3.

A tie has a similar function. It lengthens the first note by the value of the following note. The note itself is played only once and held. A half-note that is connected to a quarter-note by a tie also gives a total count of 3. Originally, the tie was used to continue notes beyond the bar in which they were written. However, today in popular music, you will also see ties used within a single bar.

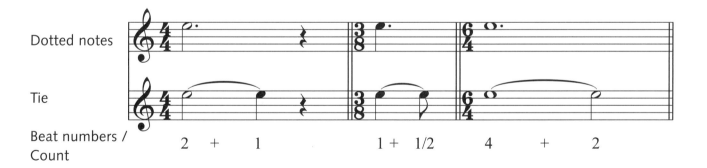

Pickup

A pickup is an incomplete bar at the beginning of a piece. The pickup is usually a quarter-note long. For example, the beginning of the American national anthem has two pickup notes.

PLAYING MELODIES

We will begin with a well known sea shanty. The word shanty comes from the French (chanter = singing). Shanties are songs that sailors would sing while they worked. Thanks to international sea travel, shanties are well known around the world. There are countless texts for them in many languages. Over the notes you will see numbers. This is the fingering for the left hand.

 **Track 09/38**

What Shall We Do With The Drunken Sailor

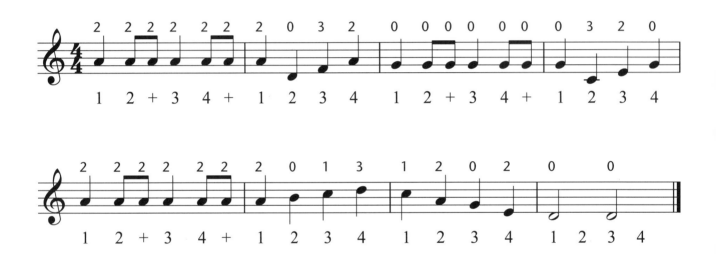

The song "When The Saints Go Marchin' In" probably stems from the 1930s, and can be played in a variety of different styles. It is especially common in Jazz and Gospel music, but there are also a wide variety of Blues, Pop and Rock versions.

When The Saints Go Marchin' In

"Whiskey In The Jar" is a famous Irish folk song which probably dates to the seventeenth century. The author of the song is unknown. After each verse, there is a chorus referring back to the Irish whiskey in the jar.

Track 11/40

Whiskey In The Jar

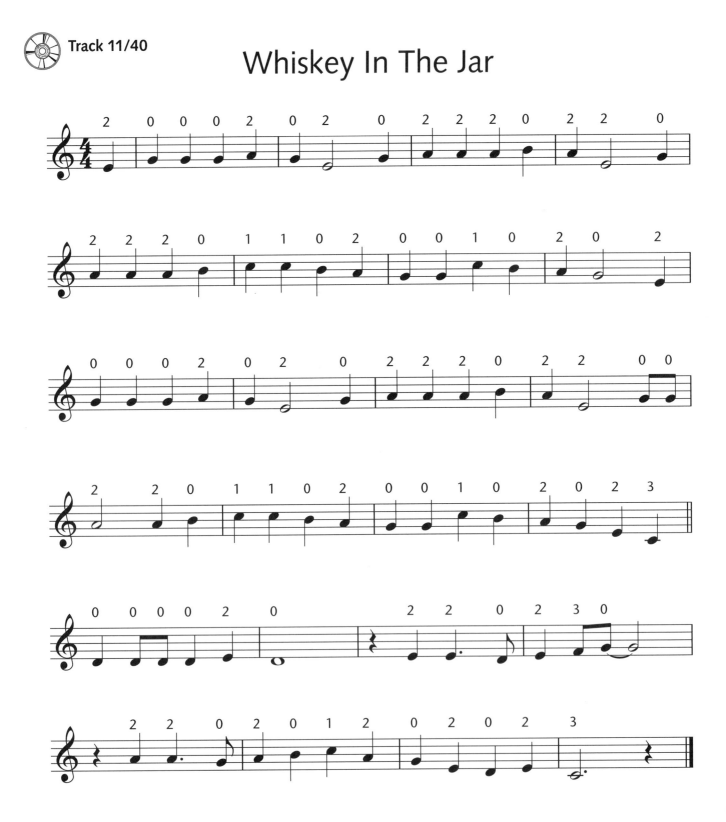

The text of the song "Banks Of The Ohio" describes a nineteenth century murder. The song must have been written shortly afterwards.

Track 12/41

Banks Of The Ohio
in G-major

We are now going to play this great song once again in A-major. Here you will see a raised natural: 'C' becomes 'C#'

Track 13/42

Banks Of The Ohio
in A-major

And now we will play the song in E-major. There are lots of sharps (raised notes) to cope with. In Version A, the sharps are in front of the notes. In Version B, they are written at the beginning of each line, which is fairly normal for sheet music. If you have sheet music from te USA, you might find that the accidentals are shown only at the beginning of the very first line. In spite of this, they apply to the entire song.

Banks Of The Ohio
in E-major

Track 14/43

To relax our hands and minds a little, here's a quieter song recognized by almost everyone in the world. Originally, it was an old English children's song. Pay attention to the meter: you have to count to 'three' in every bar!

Track 15/44

My Bonnie Lies Over The Ocean

We're going to end the section "Melodies" with the most famous love song of all time. The traditional verses from "Greensleeves" were written in the fifteenth century, and detail the lamentations of a lover. There are many variations on the text and countless recordings of the song. Careful: The parts just before the middle and just before the end are quite difficult and will only sound good if you really spread out the fingers of your left hand.

 **Track 16/45**

Greensleeves

CHORDS

The Chord Diagram (Fingering Pattern)

Chord diagrams consist of six horizontal lines that represent the six strings:

The vertical lines are the frets and the spaces between the two frets show where to place your fingers.

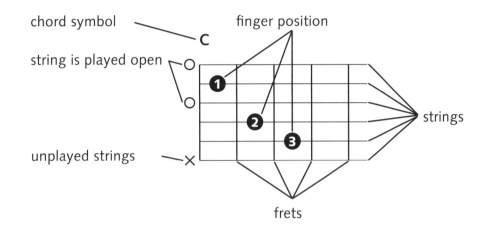

The fingers on your **fingering hand** are numbered consecutively:

1 = index finger; 2 = middle finger; 3 = ring finger; 4 = pinky finger

The **thumb** on your fingering hand does not play notes. It stays resting underneath the fret board on the neck of the guitar.

In the following fingering pattern for the E-major chord, the index finger plays the note 'g#' in the 1st fret of the g-string, the middle finger plays the note 'B' in the 2nd fret of the A-string, and the ring finger plays the key note 'E' in the 2nd fret of the D-string.

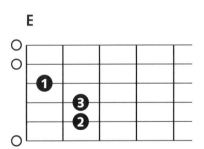

To play E-major as a fully formed chord, all the remaining strings are played open. Open strings to be played are represented in the diagram by a '0' to the left of the diagram at the level of the string to be played.

The capital letter 'E' above the chord diagram represents the **chord symbol** for the E-major chord. You will find an index of the common chord symbols on page 63.

chord symbol

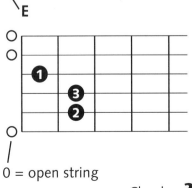

0 = open string

Numbers in a white circle show notes that can be played with the chord, but do not have to be. You can just as easily leave them out without having the chord sound incomplete or wrong.

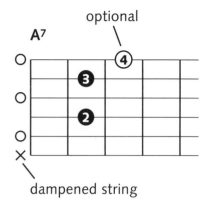

Strings which should **not be played** or **need to be dampened** are represented by an 'x' to the left of the diagram at the level of the string to be played.

If you do not start the fingering for a chord in the 1st fret but rather in a higher fret, the position of the fret is represented by a Roman numeral above the corresponding fret. Every fret represents one semitone.

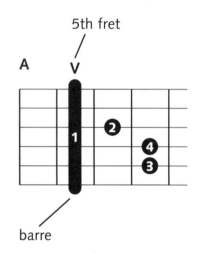

Barre chords (see page 56) are all the chords for which one finger on the left hand has to press down on multiple strings at the same time. This is represented by a black bar which extends over the strings to be played in this manner. In general, you use the first finger (index finger) to play this part of the chord, or a small device called a capo, or nut.

The First Chords

A good knowledge of the chords is important for guitarists because the instrument is first and foremost a chord-playing instrument. A flute or saxophone cannot play chords. Only keyboards (pianos, synthesisers, organs, accordions) and guitars have this amazing ability.

The guitar has six strings. The three strings (E, A and D) are called bass strings and are generally played using the thumb of the right hand. Each of these bass strings can be assigned a major as well as a minor chord. The chords differ only in the size of the third interval, called the 'third'. If the third is raised, it is a major chord. If the third is lowered, it is a minor chord.

The first chord is the easiest, and also the most important. Its keynote is the low E-string. The guitar has a standard of 4 (open) strings that belong to the E-minor chord. Therefore, in order to play a chord with all six strings, we have to change the pitch of just two strings. This is what the left hand does: the length of the strings is changed through the fingering (shortened), and results in a new (higher) note.

E-minor

The E-minor chord (short form 'Em') is the easiest to play on the guitar because you only need two fingers and they can be placed in a natural and comfortable position.

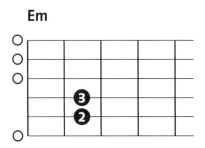

Em

E-major

We will need another finger for our second chord, E-major (short form 'E').

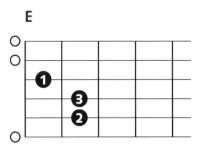

E

A-minor

E-major and E-minor have the low 'E' as their keynote. We now have two chords that have the low 'A' as their keynote. It is not a major problem if you play all six strings with this chord, but it sounds dull. Try your best not to touch the low E-string.

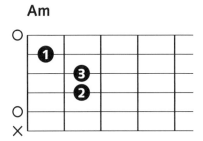

Am

A-major

The A-major chord is a little bit uncomfortable. However, it is one of the most important chords, one that it makes sense to practice as much as you can. Place your fingers vertically on the strings, and play each string individually with the thumb of your right hand. This lets you continuously test the sound of each string. Each string in a chord should create a clean, free note on its own.

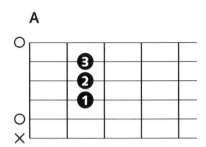

D-minor

To complete this section we have D-minor and D-major. It is not a big deal if you accidentally play the A-string in these chords, although it does not sound all that great either. The E-string, on the other hand, will make a considerable difference to how the chord sounds because the note does not fit the D-chord. It is best to hold your right hand so that you do not play the E-string.

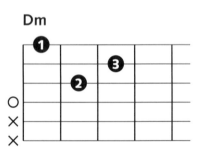

D-major

The D-major chord is one of the most popular chords for guitarists because the fingering is very similar to the normal position of your fingers. When playing the D-major chord, you should make sure that you do not play the (low) E-string and the A-string along with the other strings.

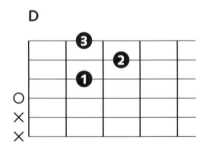

SONG MATERIAL

Songs are almost always made up of sequences of 4, 8, 12 and 16 bars. Generally, 8 bars make up a melody or a section of a melody. If a song is made up of one or more verses and a chorus, the verses generally have 8 bars, as does the chorus.

Songs With Two Chords

You can play quite a few songs using just two chords, e.g. the famous "Lady in Black" a song from the legendary British band Uriah Heep. Every beginning guitarist can start by playing this song, which uses the two simplest chords on your guitar. All of the songs on the following pages can also be played using only two chords.

The following well-known English sea shanty, whose melody you can already play, is accompanied by E-minor and D-major. The song is in 4/4 time: strum one upstroke and one down stroke per beat, 4 x per bar. If there are two chord symbols within the same bar, each chord is played for half of the bar.

Once you have got the feeling that you can play the chords rhythmically, put in the CD and try playing the song along with your 'accompanying band'.

What Shall We Do With The Drunken Sailor

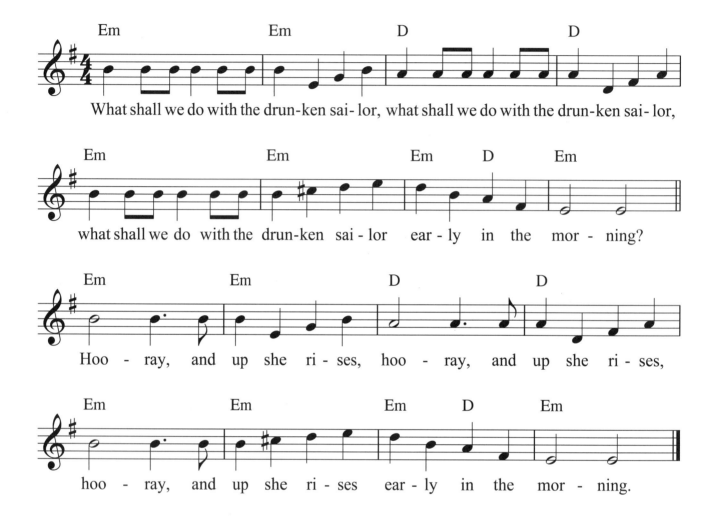

You will need a little bit of time to switch between chords at first. Try to constantly shorten the time between chord changes until there is no break at all. Remember to be patient – just keep trying. Your fingers are not at first used to the new movements, so it may take some time. Try to position your fingers all at once, that is, try to bring your fingers into the correct positions at the same time, not one after another.

He's Got The Whole World In His Hands
In D-major (in A-major)

In music, a pickup indicates the beginning of a section of melody that is positioned before the main count begins. A pickup is unaccented, and is not accompanied by a chord. You should only start playing a chord when it is positioned above the lyrics of a piece.

This song in D-major can also be played in A-major. The chords for this key are set above the piece in brackets.

TIP: In the first few song examples, the most important thing is that you switch between chords cleanly and at the right speed. Keep practicing each individual chord. A great way to do this is to imagine a chord while you are on the bus, waiting in line, or just bored, and move the fingers of your left hand to form the appropriate fingering. Do not forget: all fingers should be moved simultaneously into position.

You can also play the following song with the chords D-A. Just replace A with D and E with A. Try it out and see how it goes.

Track 20/49

La Cucaracha

La cu-ca - ra - cha, la cu-ca - ra - cha,_ ya no quie-re ca-mi-

nar; por-que no tie - ne, por-que le fal - ta__ di - ne-ro pa-ra gas-

1.

tar. La cu-ca - 2. tar. U - na cu-ca-ra-cha pin - ta!__

Le dijo a una co-lo - ra - da.__ Va - mo-nos pa-ra mi

tier - ra, a pas-sar la tem-po - ra - da.

Songs With Three Chords

It makes sense to stop a song after the chorus. Just play the chorus, then the verse and then the chorus once more. Musicians often call the chorus the A-section and the verses the B-section. So when somebody says: we are playing the song in A-B-A format, they mean: we are playing one chorus, one verse, and then the chorus once more. The pattern of chorus-verse can be repeated as often as you like. To finish, you will always want to play the chorus, sometimes even twice in a row.

We do not want this handbook to turn into a novel, so have only included the chorus and the first verse of each song here and on the CD. If you are accompanying a singer, it is best to ask how many verses he or she wants to sing.

The following song was covered by Elvis Presley among others.

Track 21/50

Careless Love

Mahalia Jackson is one of many singers to sing a version of the following Gospel song. The tempo is fast, and the song should sound loud and cheerful.

Down By The Riverside

I'm go-ing to lay down my bur - den down by the ri-ver side,_

down by the ri-ver side,_ down by the ri-ver side,_ yeah,

lay down my bur - den down by the ri-ver side,__ stu- dy_____

war no more. I ain't gon-na stu-dy war_ no more,

stu-dy war no more, stu - dy_____ war no more._____

—— I ain't gonna stu-dy war no more, stu-dy war_ no

more, stu - dy_____ war no more.

The following song is a Jewish folksong. The title means "Let us rejoice." It is a song for singing and dancing at all kinds of family celebrations.

Hava Nagila

Ha-va na-gi-la, ha-va na-gi-la, ha-va na-gi-la ve-nis-me-cha.

Ha-va na-gi-la, ha-va na-gi-la, ha-va na-gi-la ve-nis-me-cha.

Ha - va ne - ra - ne - na, ha - va ne - ra - ne - na,

ha - va ne - ra - ne - na, ve - nis - me - cha.

More Chords

Here are two more open chords for this section of the book: C-major and G-major. Now you have a total of eight open chords ready for use, all of which fit together nicely and are related to each other.

By the way: open chords are all the chords that are not played using barre fingering (see page 56), and for which you play one or more open strings along with the rest of the chord. There are even completely open tunings, in which you work exclusively with open strings. Unfortunately, we do not have time to go into these in depth here. If you are interested in the subject, you can find plenty of specialized literature in textbooks, or on the internet.

C-major

G-major

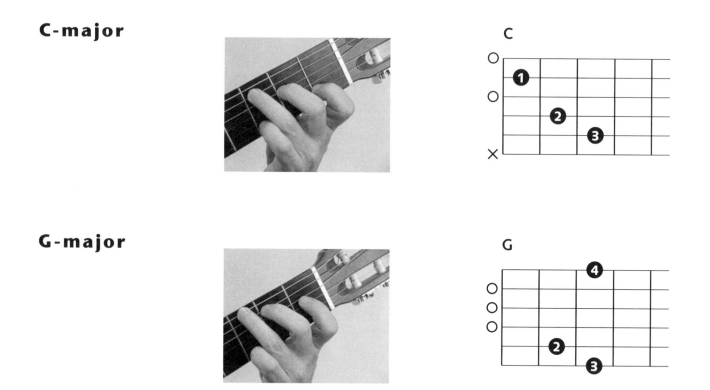

TIP: You can fudge the way you play the G-major chord to make it easier: place your 3rd finger, the one that plays the lower 'G', somewhat flat on the string. This dampens the A-string so that your 2nd finger does not need to play the low 'B'. It is even easier if you use your 2nd finger to play the low 'G' and your third finger to play the high 'g'. This trick lets you relax your pinkie finger which has a lot less strength than the others.

Here is a peaceful spiritual. The word is derived from the word 'spirit'. The texts of these songs are almost always religious, and are often meant to inspire hope in humankind.

Track 24/53

Swing Low, Sweet Chariot

Next, a classic among folksongs, covered by Jonny Hill and many other singers.

Track 25/54

Oh, Susannah

The popular Scottish melody "Scarborough Fair" was probably written in the sixteenth or seventeenth century. It was brought into the modern age by Paul Simon and Art Garfunkel on their 1966 album "Parsley, Sage, Rosemary and Thyme".

Track 26/55

Scarborough Fair

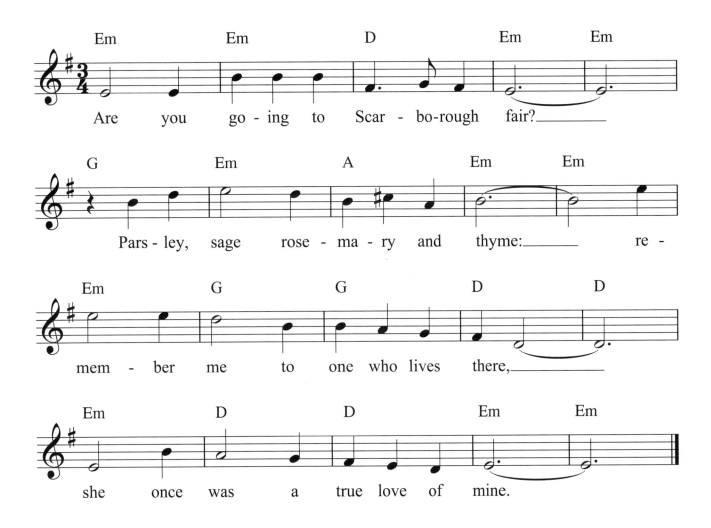

ACCOMPANIMENT

The Cadence

Maybe you have already noticed that some chords sound particularly good when played one after the other. The chords that sound best together are those whose key notes are separated by a fifth. These, the same in every key, are the chords at the so-called 1st, 4th and 5th degree. If you link these chords together, you have a cadence. The chords are sometimes also referred to as follows: the first chord is called tonic (abbreviated T), the second subdominant (SD) and the third dominant (D). The tonic assigns the key. If the tonic is the A-major chord, for example, then the song is in A-major.

Here are a few examples:

The Cadence in G-major	**The Cadence in D-major**	**The Cadence in A-major**
T SD D T	T SD D T	T SD D T
Degree: 1 4 5 1	Degree: 1 4 5 1	Degree: 1 4 5 1
Major: G C D G	Major: D G A D	Major: A D E A

TIP: When the song is in a minor key, the 5th degree can be major or minor.

The Cadence in A-minor

	T	SD	D	T
Degree:	1	4	5	1
Major:	Am	Dm	Em (E)	Am

Playing Accompaniment

You have just learned lots of interesting, definitely challenging, exercises for the left hand. Now it is the right hand's turn. It is time for strumming technique. You already know that the count '4' is very important in music. You can play 4 notes one after the other with your right hand: the thumb plays one of the three bass strings (E, A or D) and the three fingers each play one of the three higher strings. These exercises are a little uncomfortable for your hand at first because the tendons are not used to so much intensive movement – do not give up!
Generally, you pluck the strings with a thumb followed by one finger at a time. When the examples below have two fingers in the same position, two strings are played simultaneously. There are thousands of variations and ways to change the strumming order. Here are the most important:

1st variant ....thumb ....index finger ...... middle finger .... ring finger
2nd variant ....thumb ....index finger ...... middle + ring finger ...... index finger
3rd variant ....thumb ....ring finger......... middle finger .... index finger
4th variant ....thumb ....ring finger......... index + middle finger.... ring finger

It is interesting to try out percussive strumming methods for Pop songs. The thumb plucks the first string as usual. The three fingers of the strumming hand then pluck the higher three strings simultaneously. A sequence of bass-chord-bass-chord sounds great, and is usually enough accompaniment for most songs.

If you are playing with a pick: first play the bass-string, then glide evenly over the three higher strings.

MORE HARMONIES

Dominant Seventh Chords

The major and minor chords that we know now are created from the key note (1st degree), the third (3rd degree) and the fifth (5th degree) of the relevant scales. 'Third' just means the 3rd note, 'fifth' the 5th note.

If you add a lowered seventh to these three notes (from which all chords are created), suddenly you have a four note chord: the **dominant seventh chord**. This is shown by adding a '7' after the chord symbol; usually the '7' is written in superscript (e.g. D7 or D7, G7). Here are the most common dominant seven chords:

G7

This chord is easier to play than the G-major chord, and can be played with all pieces in C-major.

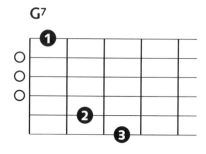

B7

The B7 chord is difficult to play. Practice the chord: you will need it again and again. The B7 chord is the dominant (5th degree) of the E-major and E-minor cadences.

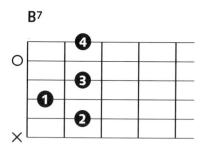

D7

A very important chord, and easy to play. You can use this chord to replace the 'D' chord in the song "Oh, Susannah" (see page 44).

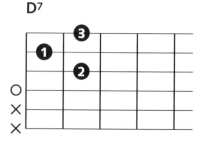

A⁷

You can easily play the chord A7 in the song "He's Got The Whole World In His Hands" (see page 37), by replacing the A chord in the D-major version with A7.

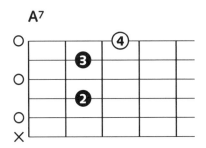

E⁷

To practice this chord, listen to the second version of the song "He's Got The Whole World In His Hands" again, and replace the E chord with the E7 chord.

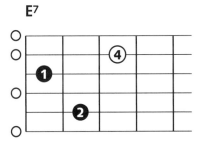

C⁷

Play the C-major chord and simply add your 4th finger to the 3rd fret of the g-string to make the C7.

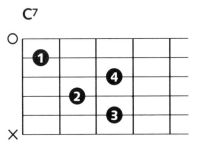

You can practice these chords in the following pieces. Once you are comfortable with the fingering, try out the songs that I mentioned in the description of the chords, and see how it goes.

She'll Be Coming Round The Mountain

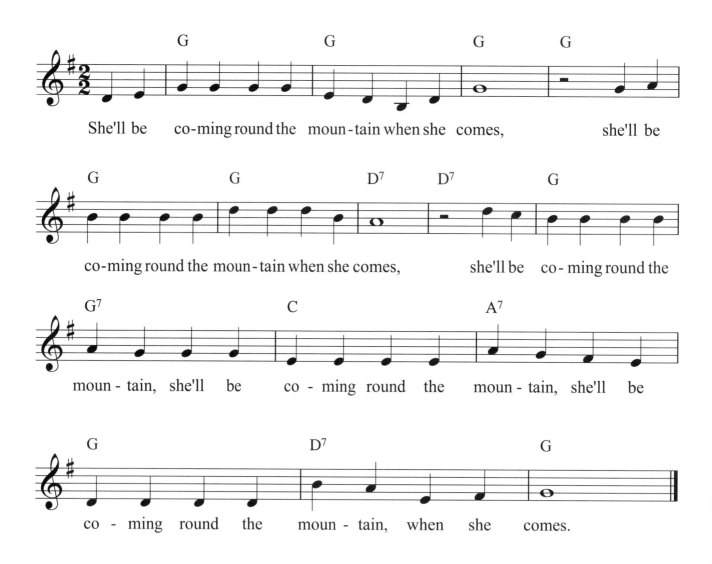

This song is fast-paced and cheerful.

Cielito Lindo

Sometimes I Feel Like A Motherless Child

You now know: E, Em, A, Am, D, Dm, G, C and 8, the so called 'open chords'.

You also know: E7, A7, D7, G7, C7, as well as five dominant seventh chords. This is quite a lot. You can accompany eighty percent of songs from around the world with the chords you already know.

Major Seventh Chords

Many things in the world come in pairs: day and night, male and female, major and minor. Even the sevenths in music can be raised or lowered, just like thirds. If the seventh, or the seventh additional note over the key note, is lowered, you have a dominant seventh chord as described in the last chapter. The seventh can also be raised, however, which leaves us with a major chord. These special chords bring colour, enchantment and that little extra something to your playing. They are especially suitable for ballads.

Major chords are written as follows: Cmaj7   Gmaj7   Dmaj7   Amaj7   Emaj7

There are other ways to show major chords, for example tiny triangles to the top and right of the letters. Or the '7' is added in with the triangle.

Cmaj7

This chord is almost as easy to play as E-minor, using only two fingers.

Cmaj7

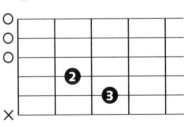

Gmaj7

Take care to dampen the A-string when playing this chord.

Gmaj7

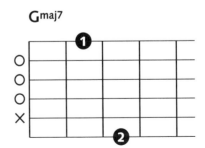

Dmaj7

You can play this chord as shown in the photo, with a small barre (see page 57), or with your fingers as shown in the diagram.

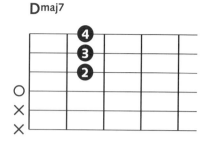

Amaj7

This chord looks almost like D7 – it is just shifted up one string. However, it is a major chord.

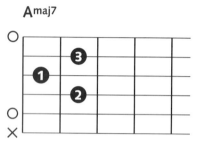

Minor Seventh Chords

I am going to repeat myself: many things in the world come in pairs. Even the sevenths in music can be raised or lowered. If the seventh is lowered in a major chord, we have a dominant seventh chord. If it is raised, we have a major chord. Raised sevenths make no sense in a minor key; they just do not sound good. The lowered sevenths are automatic in a minor key thanks to the structure of the scale. These chords also bring a lot of colour to your playing.

Am7 / Em7 / Dm7   are the most important minor seventh chords.

Am7

Another chord that is easy to play. It is like A-minor, but without the third finger.

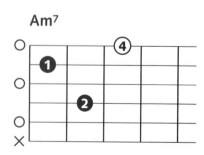

Em⁷

A great chord – you really only need the second finger.

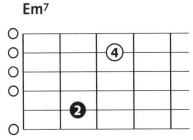

Dm⁷

It is best to play this chord with a small barre. As an exception to the general rule, bend your finger to press down on the b- and e-strings.

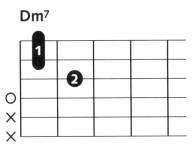

Added Notes

There are other added notes, including the fourth, the sixth and even higher partial notes. You will really only need these chords in jazz. A few examples here should be enough.

Adding the sixth note of the scale to the chord is symbolized by a small 6 in the chord name.

C⁶

One of the most useful for us guitarists, it is not easy. Place the 4th finger on the A-string in such a way that the D-string still makes a sound.

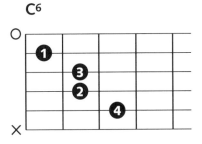

If the fourth note is used in a chord, a so-called suspended fourth is created. This chord is used a lot in modern rock music. The third in the chord is dropped, and the fourth is played in its place. The suspended fourth is symbolised by the superscript 'sus4' (sus for suspended, 4 for fourth) placed after the chord symbol.

Csus4

Make sure that you dampen the high e-string with the first finger while playing this chord.

A world-famous song with an especially interesting sequence of harmonies is "Yesterday" by the Beatles. Here are the harmonies:

Verse: C / Dm^7 / E^7 / Am / F / G / C^{sus4} / C / Am / D / F / C

Chorus: Dm^7 / E^7 / Am / G / F / Em / F / G / C / Dm^7 / E^7 / Am / G / F / Em / F / G / C

BARRE CHORDS

The Most Difficult Fingering: F-major

Try it out: play all the chords that you know without using your first finger. It is not as easy as it looks. However: once you can do that, you have begun to master the high art of the barre chords that allow you to play along the whole neck of the guitar.

Barre Fingering

When playing barre chords, the 1st finger is used instead of a capo, or nut, and is laid flat over all of the strings. The trick is 'just' playing all the chords with the remaining fingers on your hand. If you play the 8 open chords, the five dominant sevenths, and the three minor seventh chords with the 2nd, 3rd and 4th fingers, the 1st finger is always free, and can be placed across every fret on the guitar neck as an 'artificial' nut. If not all the strings are played in a particular chord, the 1st finger only has to be placed across the affected strings, which we call a small barre (see photo of Dmaj7, page 54).

I will show you the four barre chords that can be derived from the two chords with the key note E. That is F-major and F7 which can be derived from E, as well as F-minor and Fm7 which can be derived from E-minor. With 'derived' I mean that we play the chord as we learned it, but using only the 2nd, 3rd and 4th fingers while placing the 1st finger on the 1st fret across the 6 guitar strings as a nut.

The 'E'-Type Chords

The F-major fingering is nothing more than the E-chord using different fingers. The index finger takes over the function of the nut.

The F-major Chord

The key note is defined by the note on the lower E-string.

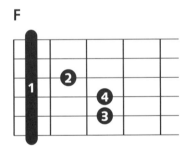

F

The F⁷ Chord

This diagram shows you the E-type dominant seventh chord. It is OK to leave out the 4th finger to make playing this chord easier.

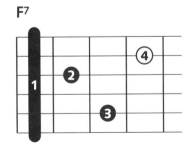

F7

The Fm Chord

This diagram shows the E-type pure minor chord. This barre chord is fairly easy to play, with an easy hand position.

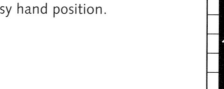

Fm

The Fm⁷ Chord

This diagram shows you the E-type minor seventh chord. This chord will also sound fine if you leave out the fourth finger. It is the easiest barre chord to play.

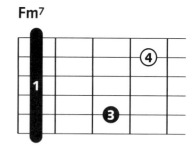

Fm⁷

We can now wander down the guitar neck using the barre fingering 'E' and produce a new chord, a semitone higher than the previous chord in each fret. You push the 'E' chords fret for fret down the fret board until you reach the 8th fret, creating 32 chords in the process. 32 different chords!!!

TIP: Some semitones can be played as sharp or flat, depending on whether the note has been raised or diminished. Example: If the F-major chord is raised by a semitone, you have F#-major. If the G-major chord is diminished by a semitone, you have Gb-major. Both chords are played in the same position on the 2nd fret. The same is true for G#-major / Ab-major on the fourth fret. This is called enharmonic equivalency, where you can switch one chord out for the other.

The four E-type chords:

Track 30

1st fret	2nd fret	3rd fret	4th fret	5th fret	6th fret	7th fret	8th fret
F	F#/Gb	G	G#/Ab	A	Bb	B	C
F⁷	F#⁷/Gb⁷	G⁷	G#⁷/Ab⁷	A⁷	Bb⁷	B⁷	C⁷
Fm	F#m/Gbm	Gm	G#m/Abm	Am	Bbm	Bm	Cm
Fm⁷	F#m⁷/Gbm⁷	Gm⁷	G#m⁷/Abm⁷	Am⁷	Bbm⁷	Bm⁷	Cm⁷

The 'A'-Type Chords

As you can see from the name, what we have here are the A-type barre chords - A-major as well as A-minor.

The Bb-major Chord

Here in the photo, the key note of this chord type is defined by the A-string.

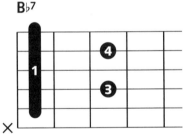

The Bb⁷ Chord

This diagram shows you the A-type dominant seventh chord. This chord is a little bit easier to play than the major-chord.

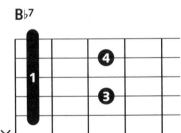

The Bbm Chord

This diagram shows you the pure A-type minor chord.

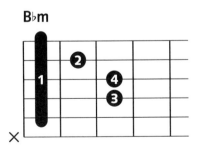

The Bbm⁷ Chord

This diagram shows you the A-type minor seventh chord. It is, as I have already mentioned, a bit easier when you simply leave out the 4th finger.

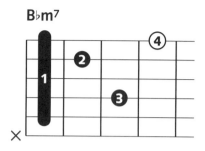

Bbm⁷

With the barre chord 'A' we can also wander along the guitar neck and achieve a new chord in every fret thatwill be one semitone higher than the previous chord.

This gives us once again a total of 32 new chords.

The 4 A-type chords:

 **Track 31**

1st fret	2nd fret	3rd fret	4th fret	5th fret	6th fret	7th fret	8th fret
Bb	B	C	C#/Db	D	D#/Eb	E	F
Bb⁷	B⁷	C⁷	C#⁷/Db⁷	D⁷	D#⁷/Eb⁷	E⁷	F⁷
Bbm	Bm	Cm	C#m/Dbm	Dm	D#m/Ebm	Em	Fm
Bbm⁷	Bm⁷	Cm⁷	C#m⁷/Dbm⁷	Dm⁷	D#m⁷/Ebm⁷	Em⁷	Fm⁷

TIP: Enharmonic equivalents also work with this chord sequence. If the C-major chord is raised by a semitone, you have C#-major. If the D-major chord is diminished by a semitone, you have Db-major. Both chords can be played in the same position on the 4th fret. The same is true for D#-major / Eb-major on the 6th fret.

You have now arrived at the end of this book. If the last few pages, in which you learnt to play barre chords, were not all that easy, you are now ready for the world of songs and accompanying them with your guitar. Even if you find barre chords too difficult, you can still accompany eighty percent of the songs out there.
So that you will feel more comfortable with your instrument, I have included a few more tips for you on the next page. After that, there is an overview of the chord fingerings that are used in the book, as well as an overview of the notes on the fret board. Have fun playing.

LAST TIPS

Playing the guitar is fun, but it can also be stressful, particularly for your fingers and wrists. That is why there are two simple, recommended hand exercises that you can do anywhere and anytime.

For the left hand, the exercise is as follows: fold your fingers into the middle of your hand, with your thumb lying across your finger tips. Then quickly spread your fingers and thumb apart, as wide as they will go. Hold the tension for a few seconds. Slowly and deliberately, fold your fingers back into the middle of your hand. This will create a small noise. My students call this exercise 'catching flies'.

The exercise for the right hand looks similar: loosely fold the fingers together, but do not press into the palm of your hand. Leave the thumb lying loosely on the outside of your hand. Now quickly spread your fingers apart downwards, or diagonally sideways, accompanied by a supporting movement of your forearm in the same direction. This exercise is called 'throwing the tennis ball'.

Speaking of tennis balls: certain types of sports such as tennis, handball or volleyball do not mix well with guitar playing. The infamous 'tennis elbow' (an inflammation of the tendons in the right forearm) is especially problematic. If you develop these issues, you will have to decide between one of your two hobbies.

The final tip is about fitness. Fitness is necessary if you want to play your guitar for decades to come without problems. The instrument does have its pitfalls. No matter whether you play standing, or sitting with your legs crossed, your spine is always bent while playing the guitar, either a little or a lot. If you play a lot while standing, you are straining one shoulder much more than the other.

That is why I, a notorious couch potato, recommend in all seriousness that all up and coming guitar heroes undertake regular back exercises, swimming, and even light weight training.

The following three points should be followed throughout your guitar playing career:

- Do not let your shoulders fall forward; keep them gently back and relax your muscles. Even when walking: shoulders back!
- Do not let your shoulders rise up to your neck while playing. This is particularly important for electric guitarists.
- Hold your right hand loosely on the body of the guitar and place the left hand on the neck without straining.

CD TRACK LIST

CHORD DIAGRAMS – OVERVIEW

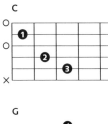
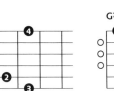
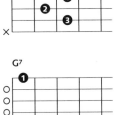
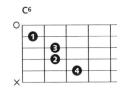
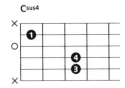
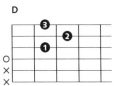
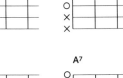
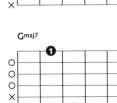
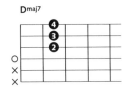
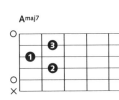
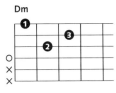
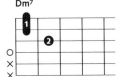
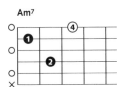
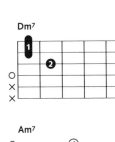
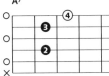
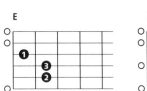
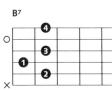

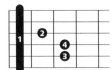
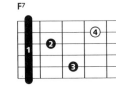
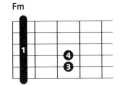
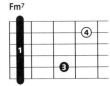
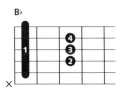
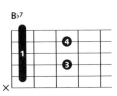
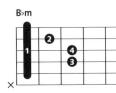

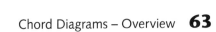

NOTES ON THE GUITAR

At the end of this book an overview of the tones on the fretboard. Below you will find all tones between the 1st and 12th fret on the neck of the guitar.

	⑥	⑤	④	③	②	①
Nut	E	A	D	g	b	e
1st fret	F	A#/Bb	D#/Eb	g#/ab	c	f
	F#/Gb	B	E	a	c#/db	f#/gb
	G	C	F	a#/bb	d	g
	G#/Ab	C#/Db	F#/Gb	b	d#/eb	g#/ab
	A	D	G	c	e	a
	A#/Bb	D#/Eb	G#/Ab	c#/db	f	a#/bb
	B	E	A	d	f#/gb	b
	C	F	A#/Bb	d#/eb	g	c
	C#/Db	F#/Gb	B	e	g#/ab	c#/db
	D	G	C	f	a	d
	D#/Eb	G#/Ab	C#/Db	f#/gb	a#/bb	d#/eb
12th fret	E	A	D	g	b	e